funny

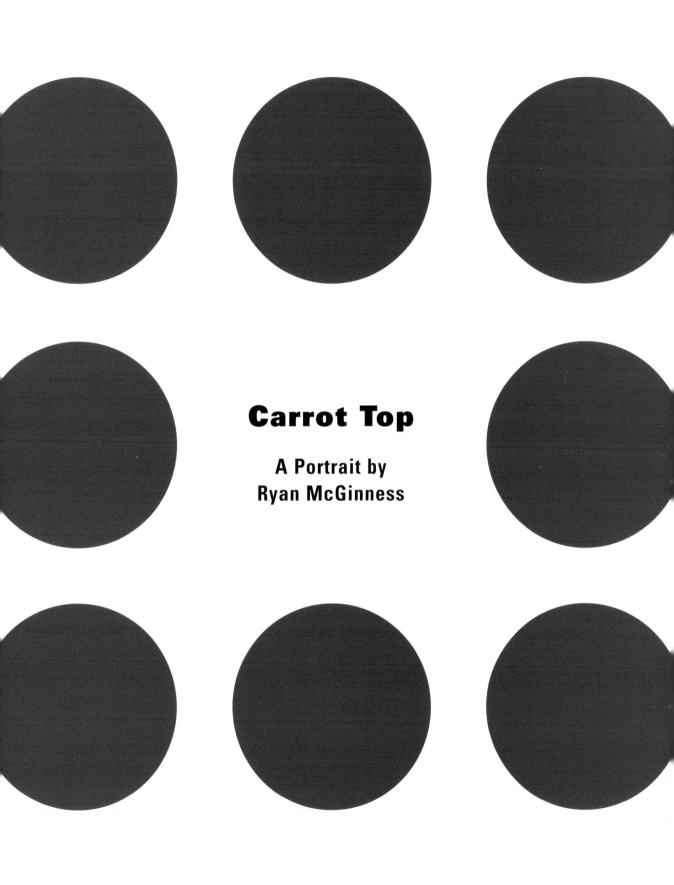

Carrot Top

**A Portrait by
Ryan McGinness**

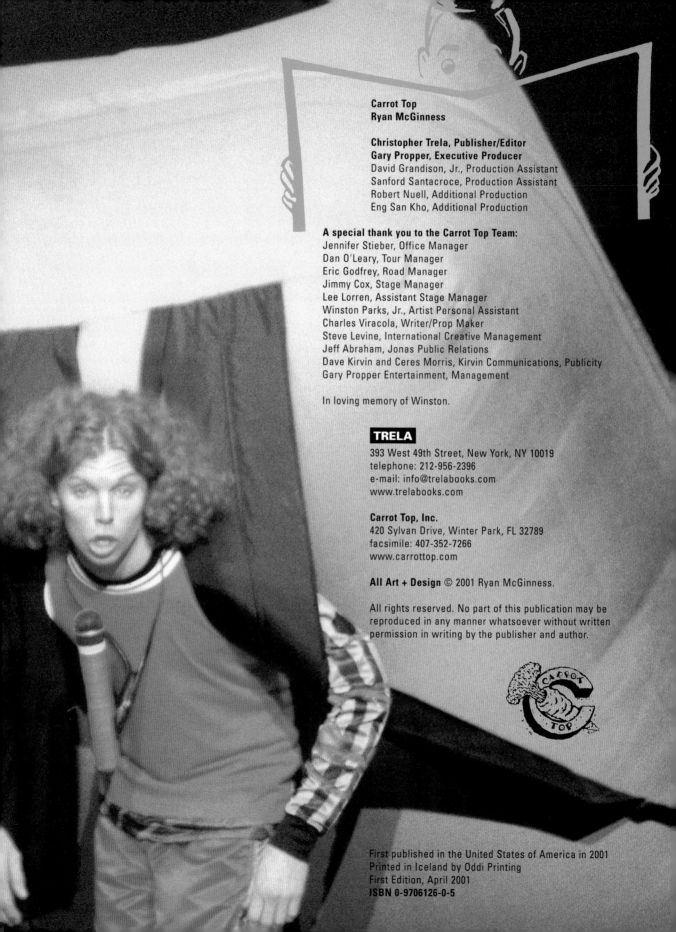

Carrot Top
Ryan McGinness

Christopher Trela, Publisher/Editor
Gary Propper, Executive Producer
David Grandison, Jr., Production Assistant
Sanford Santacroce, Production Assistant
Robert Nuell, Additional Production
Eng San Kho, Additional Production

A special thank you to the Carrot Top Team:
Jennifer Stieber, Office Manager
Dan O'Leary, Tour Manager
Eric Godfrey, Road Manager
Jimmy Cox, Stage Manager
Lee Lorren, Assistant Stage Manager
Winston Parks, Jr., Artist Personal Assistant
Charles Viracola, Writer/Prop Maker
Steve Levine, International Creative Management
Jeff Abraham, Jonas Public Relations
Dave Kirvin and Ceres Morris, Kirvin Communications, Publicity
Gary Propper Entertainment, Management

In loving memory of Winston.

TRELA
393 West 49th Street, New York, NY 10019
telephone: 212-956-2396
e-mail: info@trelabooks.com
www.trelabooks.com

Carrot Top, Inc.
420 Sylvan Drive, Winter Park, FL 32789
facsimile: 407-352-7266
www.carrottop.com

First published in the United States of America in 2001
Printed in Iceland by Oddi Printing
First Edition, April 2001
ISBN 0-9706126-0-5

HAHAHAHAHAHAHAHAHAHAHAHAHAHAHAHAHAHAHAHAHAHAHAHAHAHAHAHAHAHAHAHAHAHAH

ah-ha**hahahahahaha**

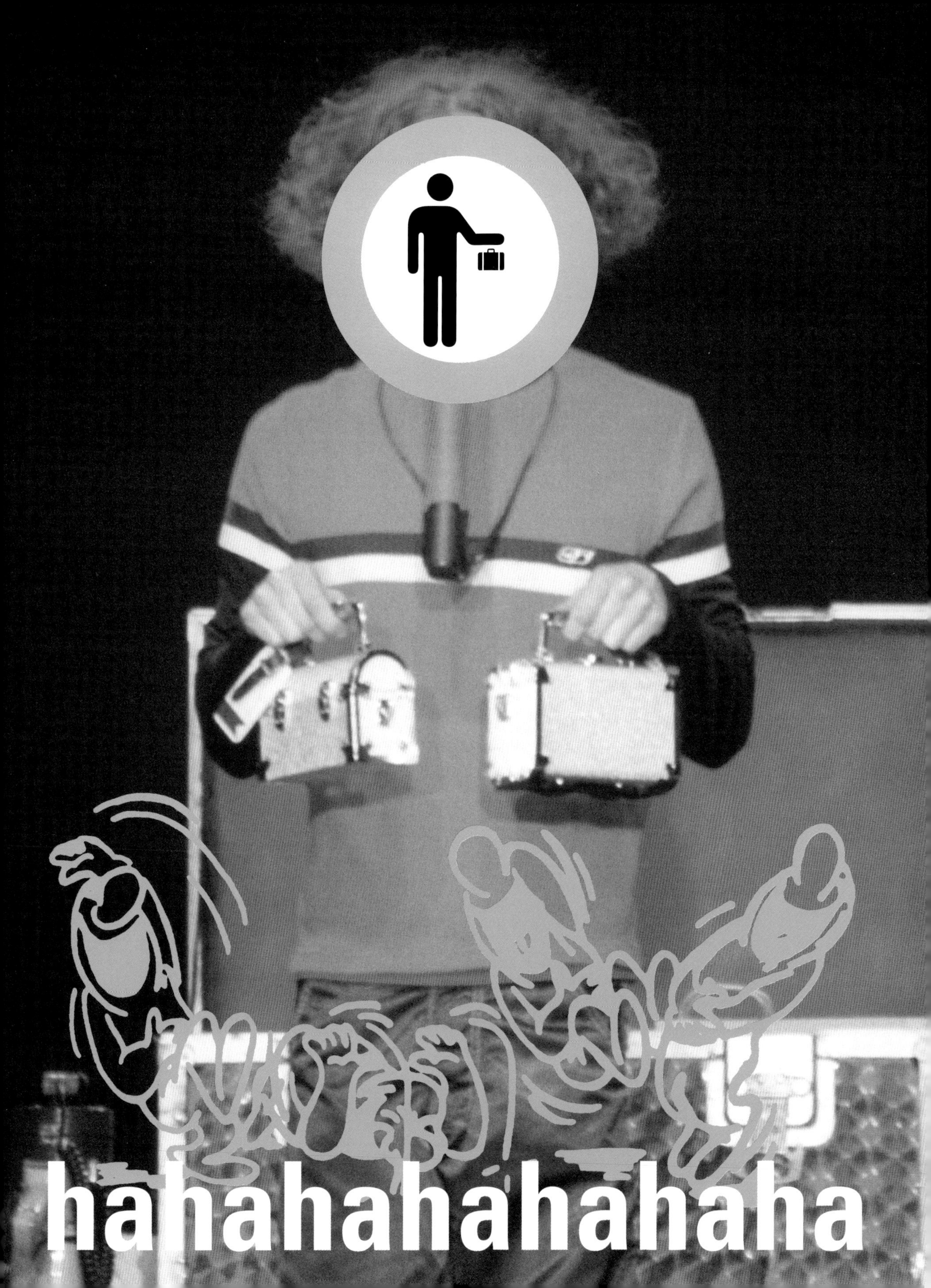
hahahahahahahaha

make**fun**

gagagoogoowwwhhhaaaaaaaaa

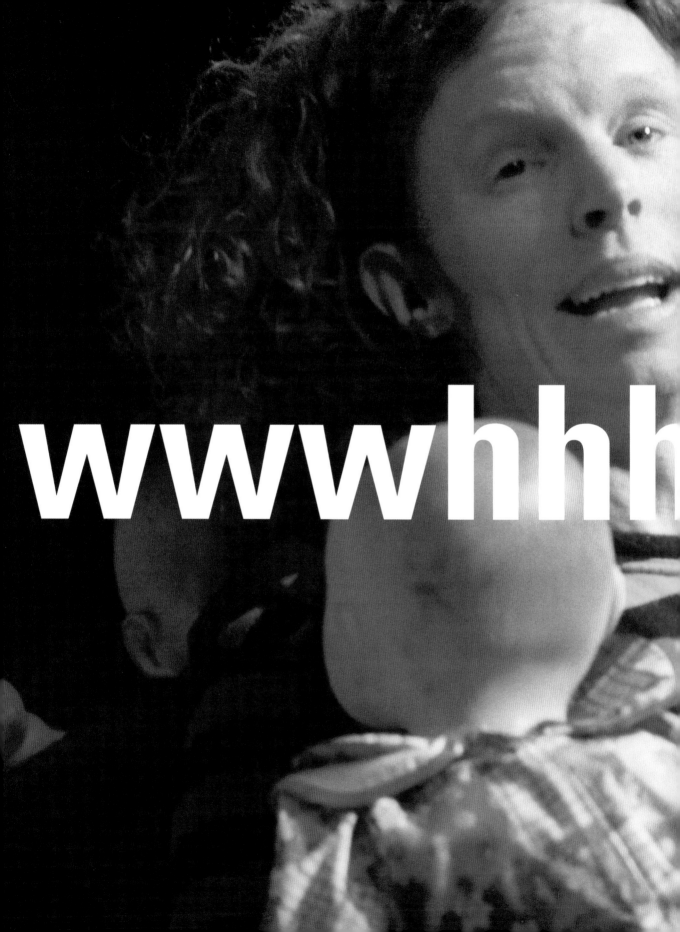

aaaaaaa

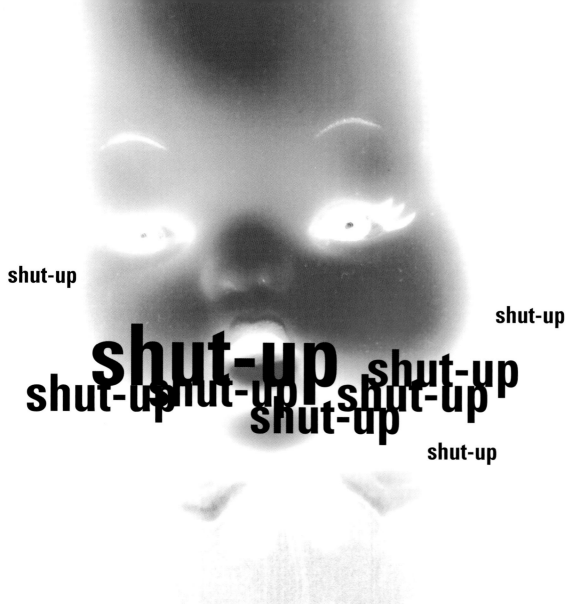
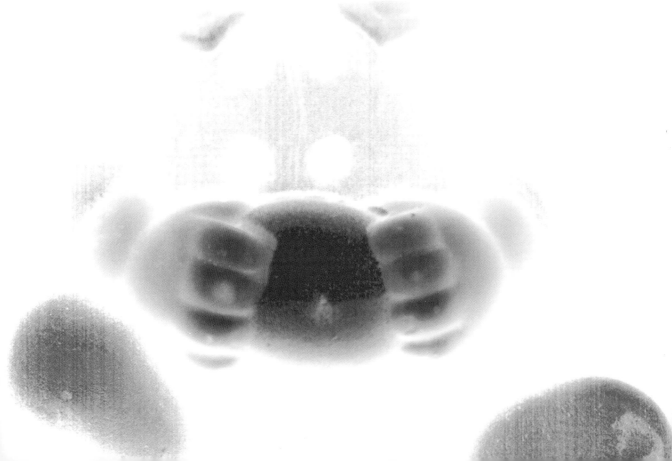

shut-up

shut-up

shut-up

shut-up shut-up shut-up

shut-up

shut-up

make**fun**of**yourself**

youarebeautiful!

chewonthis

ouch

flour**power**

ingredients

getinthecar
STOP!
GO AHEAD! TAKE A CHANCE!!!
GOOD JUDGMENT
BAD IMPULSE

inoneear

outtheother

take

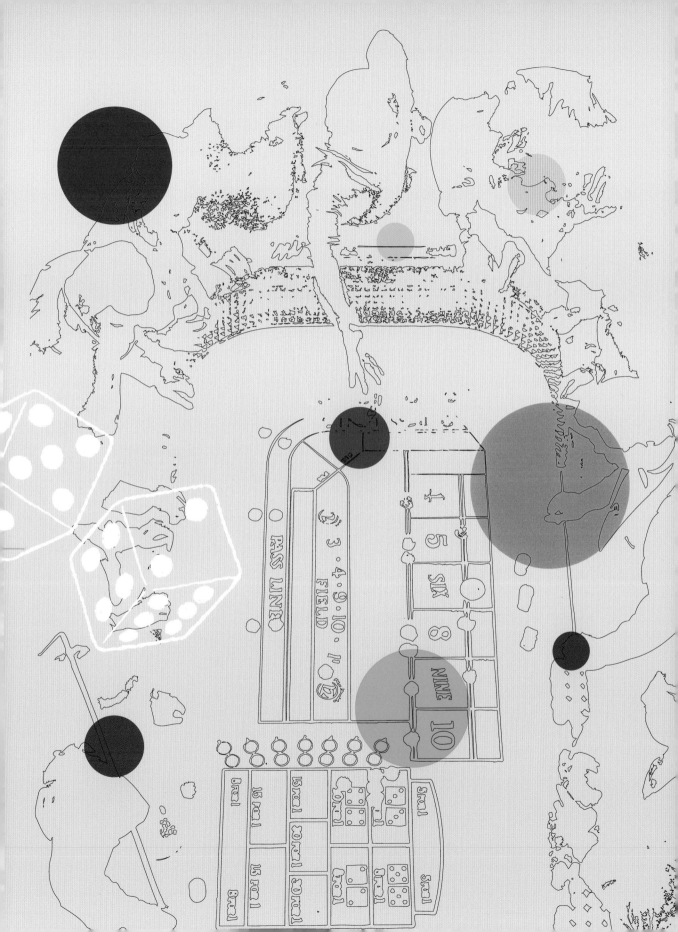

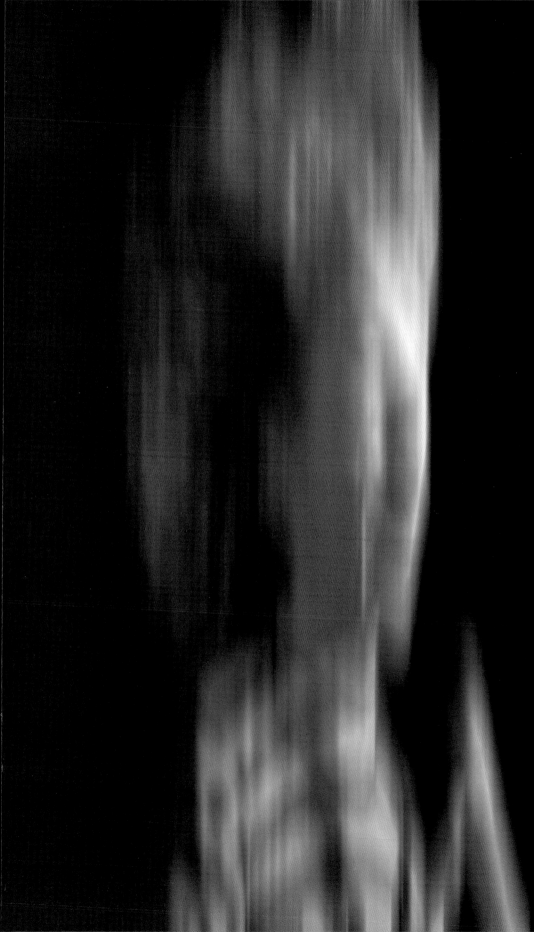

justright

carefulwhatyoueat

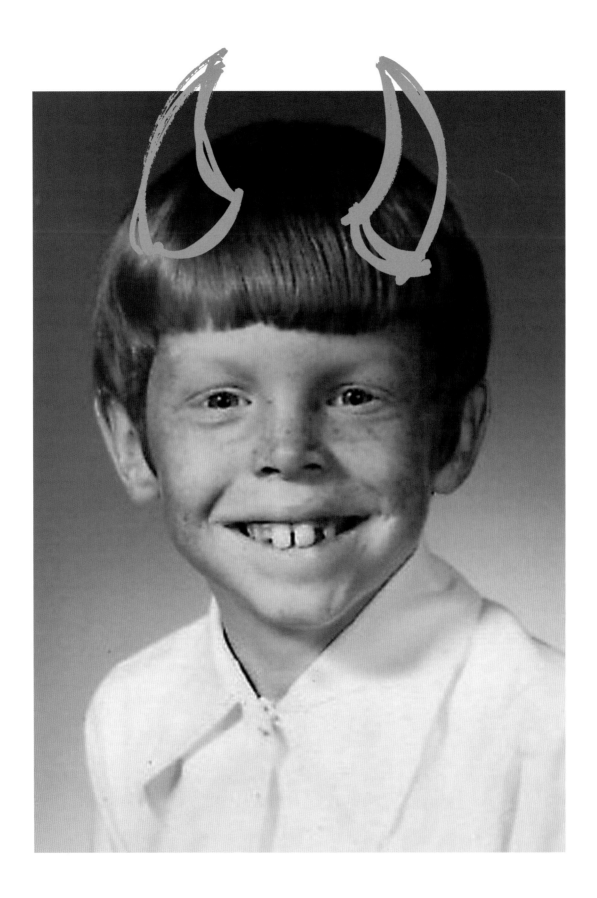

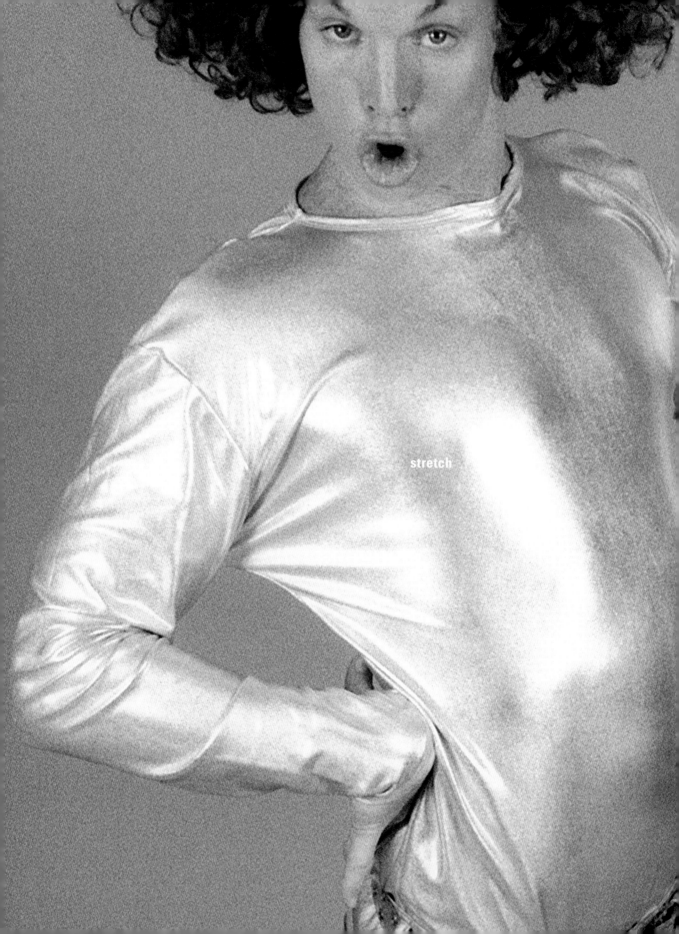

stretch

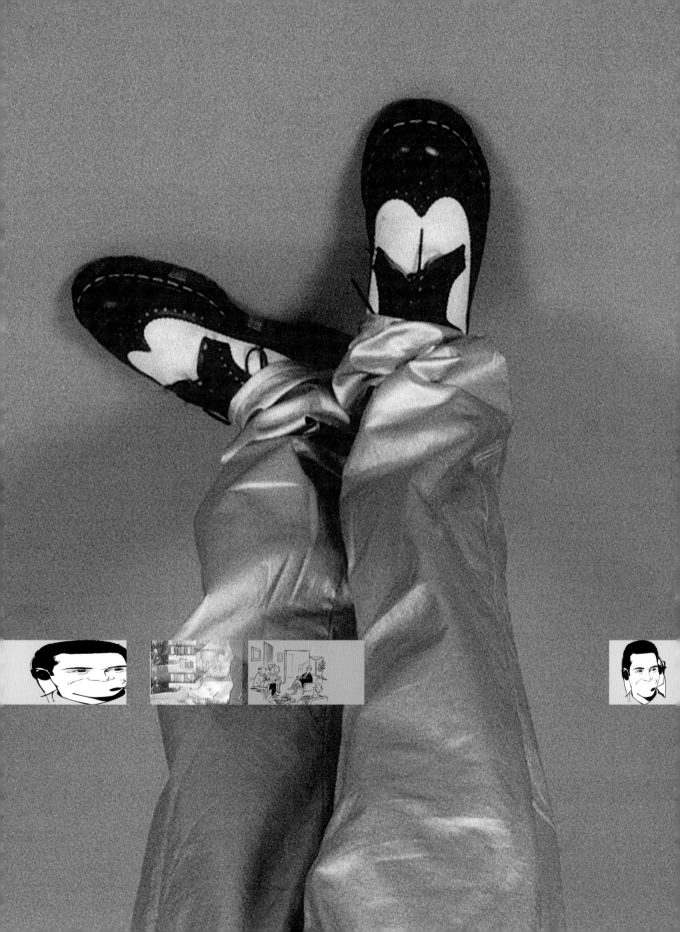

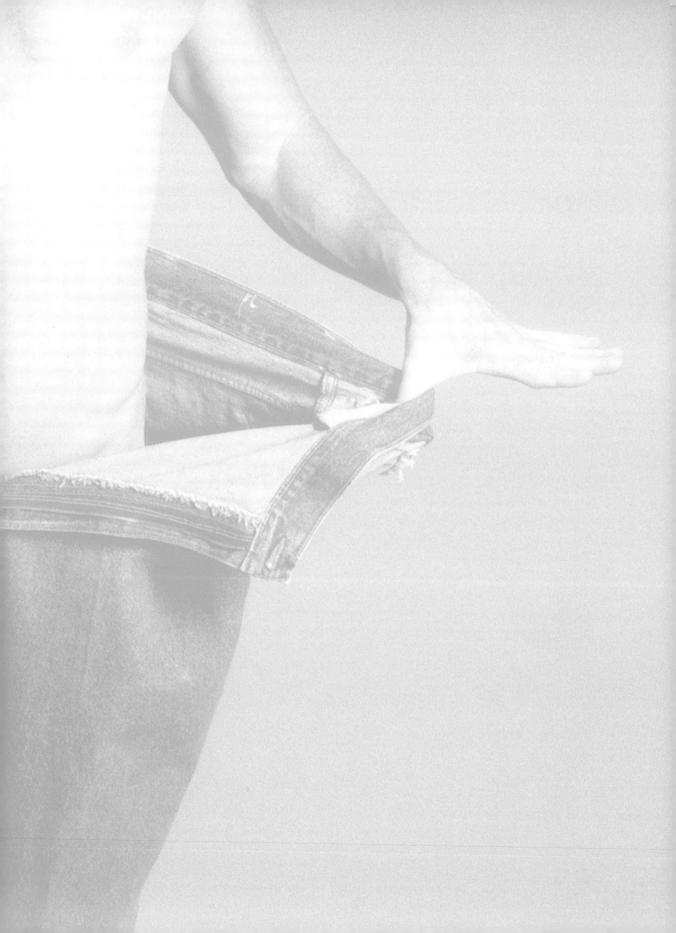

TO:
MY BEST FRIEND
IN THE WHOLE WIDE
WORLD!

FILL IN BLANK

fillinthe _____

puppetmaster

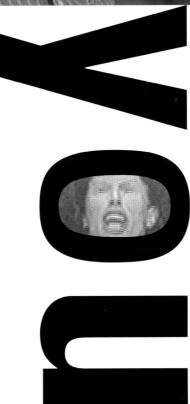

fillintheblank

fillintheblank

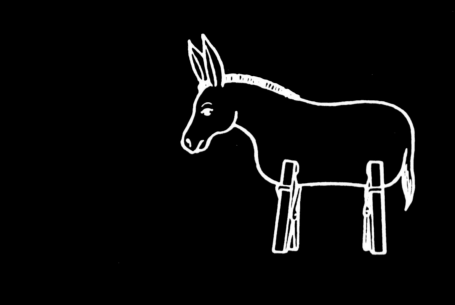

yes

PL

COMM

HE

ACE

ERCIAL

RE

con
stru
ct

dontstop

bye

PICTURE

END OF

THANKS